© Luke Osborne Jamie Parkinson

Real life experiences from the classroom to
areas that appear in your first few years of teaching.

Luke Osborne + Jamie Parkinson
Worthing, Sussex
Instagram: @Worthingdad
Twitter: @MrOzzyMaths @MrP_Teaches

Introduction
Teacher Super Powers

First of all thank you for purchasing this mini guide for Primary based NQTs. Now let me use my super-teacher-powers to work out why you've bought it! I figure it's one of the following options:

- You are intrigued as to whether our guide for NQTs is going to help
- You have followed an interesting link about improving teaching and want to read more

Let's take one point at a time...

Is the guide helpful for NQTs?

Yes! As two teachers with varying teaching experience, we have included in this short 'What they didn't teach you at Uni!' guide for NQTs lots of the basic things you can sometimes be unsure about. The entire guide is based on what we struggled with as teachers when we began our careers, and therefore what we felt would be useful to have known more about when we were NQTs or NQTs +1!

Can it allow me to improve my teaching?

This guide isn't just about improving your teaching, it is far more about giving you real life stories and strategies to use in all of the other areas which make up being a better all-round teacher. Managing your time better; frank and real behaviour management; treating lesson observations and drop ins the right way, and learning the best way to deal with parents!

Who on earth are you two?

Both Jamie and I come from a similar background. Brought up in Sussex Jamie attended Primary, Middle and High School in Worthing, and Luke attended Primary, Middle and High School in Shoreham-by-sea. We both had a love for working with children, however it wasn't a straight forward jump into a teaching degree for us both. A short story of how we came to teaching, and our careers so far, is found at the back of the book. Ultimately we hope that you find the guide helpful, and if you have any questions or suggestions for improvements please contact us through the various options found at the back of the book.

Welcome to the world of teaching!

1
Managing Your Time
Mastering the clock

Make time your friend - not foe!

A successful day in the chaotic life of a teacher will essentially be determined by how good you are at making effective use of the minimal spare time that you have. There are always a million and one things flying around your head and coping with the lessons is just the start of what you will need to achieve during the day. Do not make the mistake of letting things pile up; it will become unmanageable, uncontrollable and a stress that will be very difficult to deal with. Time management, and the clever use of little snippets of free time, will ultimately put you in good stead for the future, and give you the work-life balance that you need as a teacher.

Arrive early – leave at a reasonable time!

Depending on your school, the headteacher may stipulate an expected arrival time for teaching staff so you need to keep this in mind when deciding on how to plan your day. Since I first started my teaching career I have always arrived at school well before the school day begins, at least an hour. This has meant an early start (which some people like to avoid!) but that early start has usually resulted in me leaving earlier as well! What this actually does is inadvertently 'create' time in your day, a bonus piece of time that actually doesn't exist on your daily timetable unless you put it there. You are now a wizard with the clock, so do not waste it by having an extra cup of coffee!

This time in the morning has really helped me kick off the school day with everything ready to go, including my own mind! I believe we function more productively in the morning so an hour before school will achieve a lot more than an hour after school. You could potentially mark a large quota of books, continue planning a new unit, or maybe complete some school reports – the list of jobs is endless but this extra time will really help you plan your school day effectively.

When I have mentored trainee teachers and NQT's in the past I have always suggested this useful piece of time management to them. I have found that trainee teachers in particular find the time management aspects of the job the most challenging, particularly with the university workload on top of the school experience workload. Utilise that morning time well so that you can really ensure that you are suitably prepared for the day and week ahead.

What can you take home?

One of the best pieces of advice I would give any teacher is to take as little home as possible. Work a bit later at school maybe, because you will find it easier to motivate yourself when you are within the school environment.

That said, there is no getting away from the fact that as a teacher you will need to work at home as well school. With this in mind, you need to focus on what it is best to take home and what it is best to do in school. The first consideration here is what you can *actually* do at home. It could be that your school has an IT system where you cannot access your school server and lesson planning from home. Indeed, with the new General Data Protection Regulation (GDPR) you need to consider what the potential implications are when taking certain aspects of work home, so it is worth having a discussion with your Data Protection Officer (DPO) when you first start at your school to ascertain the ins and outs of this!

My recommendation would always be that you take home work that has a definitive ending, like a set of maths books! If you know you have 30 books to mark, you know that after they are done, that is it! If you are thinking of attacking some of that new 6-lesson-history unit at home, where would you stop? Are you going to complete one lesson plan? Two? Three lessons? All of them? Even planning one lesson properly could take you longer than the books, so I would always suggest taking home something that has a clear ending for you to aim at completing within a reasonable time frame. As well as this, I would always advise taking home something that could be completed whilst watching your favourite TV programmes too. It softens the blow!

Use of PPA

As an NQT, you will get more Planning, Preparation and Assessment (PPA) time in your first year so get yourself into good habits early on in your career! Making good use of this time is essential if you are to become a 'master of the clock!' Planning what to do with your PPA is always a great idea but be prepared for the unexpected! It could be that you need to phone a parent or deal with a problem between some children in your class, so don't always rely on your PPA 'going to plan' because it sometimes won't! Presuming that your PPA is 'normal' make sure you have set yourself some tasks that will be achievable within the time frame. Where some of your marking could be done at home, maybe consider doing some of your school-server-based work during your PPA?

In some cases, you can creatively find a way of 'extending' your PPA. If it is before/after break time, why not consider working through your break as well? Ask a colleague if they will kindly get you a cup of tea from the staffroom and this will stop the inevitable 'teacher chat' that you will get locked into and waste a good 15 minutes that could have been better spent marking, planning or making resources.

PPA time can be a substantial block of time to complete some tasks. Make sure you use it wisely. Do not get to the end of the school day wishing you had done more during this precious time! Using your break to extend your PPA can also be invaluable so make sure you plan first thing in the morning what you want to achieve – presuming everything all goes to plan that is!

Be prepared to take advice!

Managing your own time can be very difficult to get your head around to begin with so do not be afraid to ask for advice from colleagues who appear to be 'magical' in the way they complete the multitude of tasks required in a day! They can sometimes have little 'tricks of the trade' that make a big difference to their working week, so seek them out at any available opportunity.

In terms of taking control yourself, there may be times when you feel completely overwhelmed and do not know where to start. Do not let this get on top of you, and make sure you speak to your line manager. They should spend time with you to help and offer advice on how to improve in the future.

When I was head of year 7 I worked with a teacher who was really struggling with the workload. She was not a new teacher but she was a teacher who was wanting to 'redress' the work-life balance but was struggling to accommodate school work, friendships at school and a life outside of school. This was an issue that needed addressing but I was very conscious of keeping this outstanding teacher on the career path she was on. Whilst socialising at work can be encouraged at times, I suggested to her that she limited the time she spent in the staff room, particularly during her PPA, to ensure that she maximised the use of her time to the full.

We spent a lot of time looking at the workload of a teacher, from writing reports to accommodating for the unexpected, like dealing with a parent first thing in the morning. In conclusion, we decided to write a timetable for her 'free' time to see how, in an ideal week, she would be able to complete all of the work that she needed to do. Of course, sticking to this timetable rigidly was impossible, but the exercise of completing it helped her to realise that there were enough hours in the week to complete everything as long as you use your time wisely.

The success of this particular example only worked because of two factors. The first being a teacher that wanted to make a change for the better, and the second being a line manager who wanted a teacher to make a change, and was willing to invest the time in order for this happen. There needs to be a willingness from all parties if this type of dialogue is to have truly successful results.

Marking with the children

There is a lot of focus on this topic currently in the media so I will not fill this section with political jargon, but I will share some experiences that I have had of this area recently that I feel have worked!

Marking is one of the most time consuming elements in teaching and is also one of those areas that can cause the most psychological negativity! The vision of one set of books is not too daunting but when you have had four 'book heavy' lessons during the day you then have the prospect of 120 books staring right at you! At this stage, I take you back to a previous point I have made. Do they all need marking by tomorrow? Probably not, probably only your maths and English, so focus on those first and then consider a time later in the week where you could catch up with the others, maybe before school if you get in early? There is also another option that I have explored recently which I have found saves time but also makes much more productive use of the marking you are doing in the child's book.

Much of the debate in the media currently is questioning whether indeed children read what a teacher has marked, let alone use it to improve during the next lesson. I would argue the most successful teachers allow time for the children to go through their books to respond to marking but there is not always time during the busy schedule to allow this to happen. This a where a combination of approaches will help. Why not sit with individual children during a lesson and mark *with* them? It is unrealistic to suggest you could do this for an entire lesson, or get through the whole class in one lesson, but building in little bits of time for this has huge benefits for the group.

Children enjoy one-to-one time with their teacher and this focussed attention on their work can really pay dividends. I found with my year 6 English group that they preferred this way of marking because it helped them to see "exactly where they had gone wrong." I was able to target specific areas of their work with them and demonstrate in more detail what I was expecting. Not only did I see an improvement in their work, but I was also saving time from my marking load at the end of the day. By completing marking in this way, you are not 'cheating' or 'cutting corners', you are making good use of your time during the lesson with the child present, and also efficiently managing your workload in the future.

Final Thoughts

Time management is a skill, and only through positive and negative experiences will you find a solution that will work for you personally. You may find working in the evenings is better than working earlier in the morning, or vice versa, but only when you have been in the situation first hand will you really know what to expect and how to manage it.

Do not plan on completing things that do not need doing right away. Think short term. What needs to be marked for tomorrow? Could those geography books wait until the end of the week? I am not setting homework again until next week, so shall I save those books for before school on Thursday and Friday? Successful management of time relies on strategic thought and organisation. Don't let the time-consuming aspects of the teaching world take over – this will ruin your enjoyment of the other amazing parts of your job.

2
Dealing with Parents
Real life strategies

Introduction

There is no getting away from it, to be a successful teacher you will need to have some contact with the parents. Try to think of working closer with parents as an opportunity to get more success out of your children.

All parents want is understanding, time and action. Over the years I have never had a parent who has been angry with me, and this is associated with having a strong Leadership Team who deal with the bigger issues with you (or on your behalf), and also how you act and behave as a teacher. I have only ever found parents to be angry at a situation rather than you as a class teacher. That is presuming, you know you've done your job properly! Which I am sure you have.

Realising that the issue you are dealing with in regard to a parent may seem trivial to you, but appreciating that to a parent their child is obviously their world and they only want the best for them allows you to understand where they are coming from. Meeting the parents can be one of the hardest challenges for a new teacher. Some of the tips below should assist in guiding you through the murky water!

And remember:

Happy Parent = Happy Child = Happy Teacher

Receiving a message to call a parent

However your school office deliver the news, you will at some point receive notifications from the office about ringing a parent. I have no doubt that the first thing you will think about is the potential negative conversation you are going to have, even if you have no idea what the phone call is about! This is perfectly normal, so the first thing I do is ask the office if the parent gave a reason for the phone call. Sometimes you will get a detailed answer; this is the good situation where you can be prepared for the phone call before ringing back. Having an answer or an understanding of the situation, before ringing back, will make for a far more successful phone call from yours, and the parent's, perspective.

Those situations where you don't get the information before hand can be the scary ones, you will wrack your brain trying to think of a reason as to why they want to talk to you. Tell yourself the facts. Most phone calls from parents are informing you of something that is going on at home - things that are out of your control. Those phone calls are often parents looking to voice their concerns about how a situation at home could impact on their child in school. However, the blind call can be a tricky thing. You want to feel prepared for the phone call but have no idea what it is about. Think carefully about the last few school days, has the child been sad? In trouble? Have a quick chat to any other staff that work with the child as well. It doesn't take any time at all to ask a colleague a simple question. 'Has Jack in your Maths set been ok in class recently?' Don't expect a detailed answer but all you need is a yes or no.

Preparation for the phone call shows due diligence on your behalf as the class teacher, so when you ring back the parent is ultimately impressed if you do have an idea of what their phone call is about. Knowing the issue would have allowed you to formulate a plan moving forward to deal with the issue, or have an answer ready for them. Sometimes however, the phone call is just about Jack missing Tuesday Morning because he's at the dentist.

That said, if you simply do not know how to answer the parent's question when you ring back, then just be honest. Tell them what you are going to do and when you are going to get back to them with an answer. It is absolutely vital you actually do what you say you are going to do however!

Ultimately, listening is your number one tool. Most of the time parents just want the chance to talk in detail about an issue. Yes, you have a busy schedule and using your whole break time one day to listen to this call can be a pain. However putting in the effort into calls like this will help you in the long run, building relationships with the parents is vital in you achieving the best success.

Key things to remember:
1) Listen
2) Work with them
3) Manners
4) Follow up
5) Thank them for contacting you

Receiving an email from a parent

An email from a parent is a tricky one in a number of ways. We all know how reading something written on a computer screen can be read in a number of different ways, so first of all do not read an email from a parent believing they are having a go at you about something. If that is your first reaction, go and do something else for half hour and then come back and read the email again, perhaps with a colleague.

Once you've understood the email in more detail, be very careful how you reply. This obviously isn't the case for every email you send, but if you send an abrupt email in response then the parent could read negatively into the email. I usually re-read my emails about 3 times before sending to parents, and if it's discussing something more detailed or sensitive I will always ask a senior member of staff to proof read it for me before sending. These emails don't happen very often, so to keep your relationships building with the parents you need to get the one off communications spot on.

Parent Consultations

Many schools approach parent consultations in a number of ways, and some schools arrange meetings with their parents more often than others. On average, most schools will arrange parent consultations at least twice in a year, at various milestones. Usually these meetings will last ten minutes and that's it - job done!

It isn't quite that simple, however, and planning for this meeting allows for a smooth time for you, the parents and the child. Firstly you need to consider the timing. Even with a parent consultation early in the year you should have an idea as to which parents may abuse their ten minute time slot. Planning this into appointments is useful, then you don't stress that you are running behind time knowing your next appointment is waiting. This said, it is important to try to keep to the original ten minute meeting; all this preparation does is make sure you have a contingency plan if the renowned parents (renowned for chatting a lot!) push the appointment time too much.

Next in your preparations has to be what you are going to say. Parents want to know the answers to a few simple questions that you should know how to answer:

1) How hard are they working?
2) How social are they with their class mates? Who do they play with?
3) Is my child where they are expected to be academic wise?
4) What is their end of year target?
5) What can we do at home to assist their development?

Now, not every parent will be asking these questions, or even expecting these answers. Many parents are as nervous as you are about the meeting; so recognising that you are the expert and asserting the key facts about their child straight away allows you to stay in charge of the meeting - you are the expert! Most parents expect you to rightly lead the meeting, so have your information ready and be confident and honest.

Aside from the above list, it is also important to discuss their child's strengths, and how they've impressed you in areas which are not necessarily tracked ability wise. Maybe they have an incredible mind for science, or design. Perhaps they have shown a keen interest, or great ability, in a particular sport, and therefore you can suggest that they find a club outside of school and pursue it further. This part of your meeting is particularly important, especially for those children who struggle at school sometimes. Letting them know something they are good at allows them to feel a lot better about themselves. Most of the time the parents will already know that their child has an interest in whatever you've mentioned but recognising it allows the parent to know that you really do know their child very well!

When a colleague tells you a parent is a dragon...

This happens, a lot. Similar to inheriting a class from a teacher who gives a strong opinion on a child you are now teaching, teachers also do the same with their parents as well. Don't listen! You would always give a child a fresh start, so do the same with the parents. Obviously the staff member isn't trying to be unhelpful, however using what they say to then make up your own mind when meeting them is a better use of the knowledge. Terms like: needy, aggressive, difficult and time wasters are just some I hear all too often. Unless you are willing to spend your time finding out what happened in each situation and then judging whether it was fair enough from the parent, or teacher, you will become the time waster! If you follow the advice of the teacher who used these words to describe them, clearly it will just result in history repeating itself!

Who knows best?

In the section on parent consultations, I mentioned that you shouldn't forget that YOU are the expert. That is certainly the case when it comes to teaching your class and knowing how to get the best out of your class in terms the vital areas of child development and test results. However, appreciating the differences between your expert opinion on a situation and the parent's expert opinion of bringing up the child is very important as well. You need to realise that the parent ultimately knows best for their child, but not with all areas. This is where your school's policies are important. You have a set of rules that you are expected to follow and therefore it is your job to follow those policies.

If a parent request you don't sit their child with another child for sensible reasons, it can be a pain. But this is because they've good reason, and very rarely just simply because a child doesn't like someone. It could be that for the whole previous year a child has sat with their best friend and hasn't made as much progress as expected, or that the parent has been repeatedly told that they are always chatting too much in lessons. In these smaller situations, go with the parent.

However, if the parent's request for how you should be doing something differently to what you are doing is something you consider unfair, or against your expert opinion, stay polite and tell them that you are following the school's policies as you should do. However, do not leave it there - that will not be the result the parent's want because it simply isn't good enough. Tell the parent you will, however, speak to the senior leadership (preferably a deputy or head teacher) about their concerns and get back to them. There is no doubt that the senior leadership will support your point of view and the school's policies, however there will be times where they may give you advice with how to proceed or allow you to stretch the policy slightly. It is important you know that your senior leadership have the control over altering and tweaking how policy is delivered in their school, and working on a solution together with them allows for the best result for all. When getting back to the parent, you can be honest and tell them how the conversation with the senior leadership went. If they are still not happy, you can advise them to make an appointment with the headteacher to discuss it further. You have attempted to find a solution to suit everyone which the parent should appreciate, however ultimately you cannot solve every situation!

Final thoughts

Preparation is vital for success when dealing with parents, as is knowing the child. As an NQT, or a inexperienced teacher, you must seek advise from colleagues when stumped by a parent. This must not be seen as a weakness or a failure! You cannot expect to be an expert at dealing with parents, you can never predict how a parent will be therefore it isn't easy to ever be such a thing. Just remember, parents will appreciate honesty in terms of you not having an answer straight away so don't be afraid to find support.

You are a great teacher and developing healthy relationships with parents will allow you to become an ever-better teacher.

3
Managing Behaviour
No gimmicks!

Introduction

No matter what your experience in the lead up to your NQT year there will always be that moment where you are first stood in front of a class, 30 pairs of eyes transfixed on you, waiting for you to begin the process of imparting knowledge. It is this moment that represents a crossroads for many children. Their subconscious mind will decide whether to behave or not depending on which path you as a teacher lead them down: will you encourage intrigue, or will they sense the nerves and prey on your inexperience?

Rule 1 – YOU are in charge

You will be terrified when you first lead your class from the playground to the classroom, but this is where it all begins – the foundation of respect that will ultimately determine the road your class will lead from. First of all, ensure that the children are lined up properly. Sounds simple, and obvious, but if you lead them as a rabble they will behave as such en route! Remember to outline the expectations. YOU will lead. Why? It will stop the children running and it also outlines the strength of you as their leader. You lead the class, you teach the class, you are in control of the class. Yes, you will be terrified, but those children will never know how terrified you are or the psychological line of respect will immediately be challenged.

Laying these foundations from day one is crucial to the success of you as the leader of your class. Developing that high level of respect will allow you to relax at certain points in the year and then 'reign in' when necessary. With no foundation laid early, you will struggle to establish firm boundaries from which your children can work from.

Rule 2 – YOU will win any confrontation

Some children will present exceptionally challenging behaviour at times but the key element will be your reaction when they do. If you try and 'shout a child down' it will not always work, and if it doesn't, where do you go from there? Shout louder? Don't get me wrong, there is a time and place for the use of the voice. Indeed, it has been one of the most useful tools I have had in my locker, but it must be reserved for those moments where it can have absolute impact, and you must always be in control. Shouting as a reaction will have little effect. Shouting to make a carefully considered point can be quite powerful.

When a child is particularly confrontational, the calmer you are with the situation, the calmer the child will become, as a general rule of thumb. In the instances where this is not the case, you may simply have to send another child to alert a member of SLT to the situation. This is not an admittance of defeat but more a show of solidarity amongst the staff. You are saying to the child "you are simply not doing as I have requested, the learning of the other children is now being affected, and I want to teach my class. If you are not going to follow this, you will need to leave."

Rule 3 – Reverse psychology is a winner!

Ask yourself the following question: why do children present challenging behaviour? Now, not every case is the same of course and there could be many issues that the child is dealing with that can lead to this, but most children will display a challenge because they are desperate for attention, be it positive or negative. Some children live in a world where they receive very little, if any, positive attention from their families. All they are used to is the negative attention they receive and so they know no different. Shouting at these children will have little, if any, impact, and the result will be a 'no win.'

Why not reverse the process? Diffuse the challenge, continue the lesson, and then afterwards spend some time with that individual, discussing with them the result of their behaviour. I have found this tool one of the most effective ways of winning over those children that present the most challenge. They are challenging you because they are desperate to be liked and they have no idea how else to encourage such emotions. With this in mind, have a look at the following script, a conversation I had with a year 6 child:

Teacher: let's take a look back at the lesson. Can you see why you calling silly things out was wrong?

Child: no.

Teacher: ok. Put yourself in my shoes. Do you think I find it easy to teach the class when you are behaving like that?

Child: *(long pause)* suppose not.

Teacher: do you know what? I'll be honest with you. I actually find you quite entertaining, and what you are saying is very funny...

We both afford a wry smile...

Teacher: ...but you need to know where the line is between making the lesson and classroom a fun place to be, and where you are being disruptive to the learning of the class. Can you see where I am coming from?

Child: I think so...so am I allowed to have a laugh then?

Teacher: of course you are. As long as you know where the line is. This game is learning. If your learning or the learning of the other children is affected, you have gone too far. Do we have a deal?

Child: yeah!

Teacher: right. Tomorrow, we will start again. You will really upset me if the same thing happens again because we have just had an adult conversation and you have been brilliant. If the same thing happens again I will not be angry, I will be really upset, because I will feel like you don't care about upsetting me. Now go and kick a football around – I look forward to seeing you tomorrow.

The key element for success here was differentiating between being angry and being upset. By displaying a 'human' element to the situation it empowered the child. They had the decision to make. Did they want to upset the teacher that they had been craving positive attention from, or did they want to revel in their own success and receive the positive rewards?

Was the child perfect afterwards? No, not at all, but I never had to have the same conversation again and the child went on to have a superb end to the year. They did well, and I got a bottle of wine! I think they call that 'win-win...'

Rule 4 – Every day is a new day

You may think this is obvious, but I have worked with many trainee teachers who have struggled with this. Putting this rather simply, 'holding a grudge' against a child is one of the worst things you can do. It will have all sorts of problems attached and will encourage the disruption within the classroom to escalate further.

I had a conversation with a TA recently. She asked me the question "have you ever taught a child that you don't like, because you seem to get on with everybody?" My reply was just a categoric 'no' because my mind just doesn't work that way! Yes, we all have those days where some children drive you completely bananas, but I never get to the point where I don't like them!

No matter how bad your day has been, no matter how much pressure you are under, no matter how tired you are, the children can never be on the receiving end. Everyone has a bad day, children included, so it is important to keep that at the forefront of your mind. Just because they did something ridiculously annoying yesterday does not mean you need to continue chastising them today. Give them a chance. Allowing the opportunity to improve following a mistake will ultimately give you the best reward for that child to succeed in the coming days.

Rule 5 - Be ready to say sorry to a child

Now some may frown at this one but experience has taught me that the more 'human' you are with the children in your class the more you can have them eating out of the palm of your hand! Some days in teaching are incredibly intense and stressful and this can lead you to taking out vented frustrations in the wrong direction. You may be a little short with a child, you may have jumped to a conclusion that actually ended up being wrong.

Rather than holding the 'high and mighty' stance take the approach of being honest and apologising. This works on so many levels. Firstly, you are telling the child that everyone makes mistakes and it is your reaction to them that will ultimately determine the person you become. Secondly, you are demonstrating a mature approach to a situation. Finally, you have created something that you can keep in your locker to bring out at an appropriate time! "You have really upset that other child today and now you are refusing to take responsibility...do you remember that time that I made a mistake, and I apologised for it?"

The art of a good apology should never be underestimated. Take the opportunity to be honest with your class whenever you can. You will find addressing behaviour that involves a lack of honesty much easier to handle if you yourself have demonstrated that honesty in front of the children.

Rule 6 – Share in a Child's Success

You may think this is an obvious statement to make but when we are discussing this we are going further than the positive praise that you are trained to give children in terms of celebrating their success.

So many children display challenging behaviour because they are only ever used to negative attention at home. This bad behaviour can often lead to negative attention at school as well, so one of the most successful ways to improve upon this is to focus on the positive elements in a school day, no matter how small they may be.

What should you be praising? Well this will differ from child to child and the extent to which their behaviour has become a problem, but you should be focussing on something small to begin with. During my NQT year I worked with a child who used to really struggle on the playground at lunchtime and was often in trouble. I had real problems with this as it was fairly frequent and it would make the lesson after lunch so much more difficult. I ran out of ideas until I stumbled across something so easy! When I did the register after lunch instead of the children answering with 'Yes Mr P' I asked them to briefly tell me what they did at lunch. I had some varied responses from 'football Mr P' to 'we played a pretend chef game Mr P' but this was a great way to explore what the children had done, who they had played with but also *praise* certain elements of behaviour from those that had really enjoyed their time together. The child I always had problems with clocked this, and he wanted to be a part of it. We didn't solve everything all of the time, but we certainly made things a lot easier. He developed a desire to do the right thing to earn the praise during the register – simple, but very effective.

As a general rule, children will behave better when they feel they are being treated fairly both in terms of the bad things they do but also the good. Picking up on small changes in a child's 'everyday school locker' can make a big difference. It might be an improvement in handwriting, it might be walking more sensibly in the assembly line, it might be an improved performance in an academic subject – focus on anything that has been improved but make sure that the child knows you have noticed it.

Some children, particularly those that are only used to negative interactions, can find the sudden use of praise complex to handle. Experience tells me that the art of delicacy is key here! Take the child to one side to begin with to discuss their successes with them personally, and then gradually increase this praise and celebrate success in front of the whole class, if you deem it appropriate to do so.

Final thoughts

Managing behaviour is one of the most challenging elements of being a teacher, and it will be particularly difficult in your NQT year. Always keep in your mind that the children are waiting for YOU to set the boundaries and for YOU to maintain them. The minute you let that standard slip will be the minute they will attack from all angles. The greatest days you will have as a teacher will be those when you let the reigns go a little…you can only allow this to happen when you know where you need to reign them back to later on.

4
Lesson Observations
Don't stress!

They really don't need to be scary

Lesson observations don't have to be a scary thing. You've got this far after endless of the things, however it is a little different when you are holding your first official teaching position. At university you could use your strengths and weaknesses, especially the weaknesses, to produce an excellent essay! And yet in your new job, you fear that it will affect your reputation within your school. Well I say to you now, that is nonsense!

I have been there, terrified about my first observation. Up all night preparing, over preparing - looking for a wow factor all of the time. Nervous to the pit of my stomach, sweating, being incoherent sometimes. Then I arrived in class, throughout the entire observation I was rigid. I was so concerned about my body language and movement around the classroom, I seemed to replicate the movements of a praying mantis after an espresso. So the advice is: you must take a professional and practical view on what observations really are for, and how you can use them for your benefit.

Don't doubt your everyday teaching!

First of all you would not have been employed if the Senior Leadership Team didn't believe in you. You have been hired for a reason, the school must see potential in you! This is the key, they have not hired an NQT because they see you as the finished article. The school has hired you as they see the potential in you as a teacher, and also because you are cheap. Don't be hung up on being cheap though, we all had to start somewhere and the school wouldn't have hired you just for monetary reasons!

You must learn to take lesson observations as an opportunity to get better at teaching. Teaching is an ever changing environment, and we can all ALWAYS get better. This is why it is important not to put on a 'bells and whistles' lesson which WOWs the observer. That might be what your school is after, and after putting on this incredible and fake lesson you might get this glowing report about how wonderful you are. It will leave you feeling marvellous, and you will start to think you know are the best teacher ever and all the old hacks in the school need to follow your lead. That feeling might make you warm inside for a little while, but deep down you will know that your everyday lessons are never anywhere near that standard. The problem with this situation is that you won't get real feedback to make real improvements as a teacher.

Lesson observations are not to make you look bad, not for you to show off the world's best lesson, but to allow you to get better at teaching. Don't get sucked into the negative. If you are doing something wrong regularly in lessons, but don't realise it is wrong, then that surely needs to change. It won't change however unless you've taught a normal lesson for an observation!

You get my point. That said, I do appreciate the fact you will want to be prepared slightly more than usual; you might be slightly hotter on your movements around the room or behaviour strategies are slightly tighter when you've a visitor. Obviously that is a normal reaction to being watched, once someone said that you are at your best when you know you are being watched. If only that somebody had told me how many colleagues were watching me dance at the staff Christmas do...

Preparation

So, I've just told you not to fret and to just deliver a normal lesson for your observation. But you are still fretting and want to know what you can do to ensure your lesson is as tight as possible, even though you are now convinced that you don't need to perform a WOW lesson. That is perfectly normal, so let's talk through a few key things to think about when preparing or teaching a solid lesson. Starting with two key areas that need to be in place before the lesson begins.

Prior Knowledge and Resources

A.	Research your subject knowledge thoroughly
B.	Are the resources fit for purpose?
C.	Ensure some interaction

Starter

A. Be Organised
B. Start Promptly
C. Get Children involved early

Pitch of Lesson

A. Is it challenging enough for higher ability?
B. Is there appropriate support for less able?
C. Is the lesson age appropriate?

Behaviour Management

A. Tight
B. Consider ethos of your class
C. Follow behaviour management

Awareness of Needs

A. Are you moving the class on as needed?
B. Is progress obvious?
C. Are you aware of those struggling?

The Plenary

A. Effective conclusion
B. Can children demonstrate learning?
C. Does the lesson lead into a follow up lesson?

These are all things that as an NQT you should already know about, however sometimes it is usual to see a list in front of you.

Your books

Most observers will take a keen interest in your book, which is part of reason why teaching a one off wonder lesson is a little daft. Your books will show how much pride the children have put into your teaching, how effective your marking has been and generally how the children are progressing. With any lesson observations which occur after Christmas, progress in the children's books should be obvious.

It always happens though, the observer looks at the 2 books, out of 32 possible books, that you didn't want them to look at. Your reasons for why you don't want them to look at them are probably varied, but don't panic - they should understand you teach a variety of abilities. Whatever the standard of work in a child's book, they are still looking for progress and should completely appreciate that progress varies from child to child.

Make sure your books are marked, as per the school's policy, within the past few lessons at worst. I am certain if you looked at the observers books they will not be marked up until the past hour, and if they are that is not the expected in the real world.

Teaching away from your plan

Sometimes what you've got planned just doesn't work out. It could be that the children act differently as they know there is someone acting awkward in the back of the class room, or it could be that you are not as relaxed as you usually are. It could even be that the plan for the lesson just isn't any good and you didn't see it coming until you taught the lesson. This happens sometimes in normal lessons, therefore it might happen in an observation as well.

Use it as a positive opportunity. Things going wrong? Then deal with it! You should have probably considered some things that could go wrong before, therefore might have an idea on how to correct it. Think on your feet. Have all the children misunderstood the task? Do you have a record amount of hands in the air asking for support? Don't frantically run from child to child. Bring them all together and re-clarify the task using different vocabulary and in a different way. If some children have got the task, and are cracking on, then let them continue and check in with them when everyone else continues. It isn't always this simple, but thinking fast is what us teachers have to do every single minute of every day. Anything could happen at any moment with 30+ children in the room, and so you make these decisions confidently already. This is no different.

Behaviour can fluctuate in an observed lesson as well. As we know with difficult behaviour, there is quite often influences out of our control at play. Therefore it might be the fact you've someone different in the room, it might be that they sense you seem a little more highly strung than usual. The vital thing to remember, is deal with behaviour issues the same way you would usually. Do not suddenly become extra strict, or let things go. You stay consistent with the way you run your class, and in line with the school policy.

I usually let some children know if a visitor was coming in for varied reasons, sometimes it was because I had children in my class who struggled with changes such as an unannounced visitor. For this reason I would give them a heads up, sometimes I would tell the whole class and the conversation would go something like this:

Me: Oh guys, I thought I'd mention we've Miss Smith coming into visit us in English this morning.

Pupil: Why are they coming in?

Me: They just want to see the kind of things you get up to in English and have a look at some of your work. They might even get you to explain to them what you've been doing recently.

That is all that is needed. In a way you have relaxed the situation because the children are aware of the visitor and that the visitor is only coming in to be nosy and see what they get up to in a lesson. Let's be honest, that is all it is! Not looking to bring you down, just a chance to be nosy and see what you could do better, to improve as an educator.

The Lesson Observation results

When being observed, most schools don't grade like they used to. It is quite rare for schools to grade lessons as requires improvement, good or outstanding. This is because of the alterations in Ofsted expectations. This doesn't mean your lessons won't be graded in some way however, but don't get hung up on them. If you have delivered a decent 'normal' lesson, and your observer has identified your strengths and weaknesses then you can use this to improve for next time. Remember, keep your lesson observation like a slightly tighter normal lesson - this will allow the observation feedback to be most useful. Your observation is a chance to learn and improve as a teacher, not a chance for someone to make you feel like a rubbish teacher.

Final thoughts

Don't panic about lesson observations, they are there to make you a more accomplished educator - not to trip you up. Teach a real lesson. How can you ever get better if you become a completely different teacher when you are watched? You can't. No one knows it all, and you will disagree with some opinions at times - it is a professional environment so that is completely normal. Don't over think it. Don't consider the lesson observation as a way for your school to trip you up, they want to see you in action and work with you to then get the best out of you.

5
The Authors
A little bit about us

Luke Osborne

I was a little lost before finding teaching as a career, attending two colleges whilst studying a whole host of random subjects. It took a long while before I accepted that my calling was teaching. I always felt that I would make a good teacher however I had very different visions for my future careers.

Sadly, I spent too much time socialising at college and studying subjects which ultimately didn't assist me in my career today. However, I did finally complete a sports coaching course at Chichester College which led to me working for a sports coaching company. This company delivered PE lessons to schools who lacked teachers who were keen to lead PE in the curriculum.

I really enjoyed the role, but I longed to be working as a class teacher - not teaching PE all day every day. This came from a position where I was visiting upwards of 6 different schools a week, and therefore it allowed me to see how the variety of schools were run and how I would like to develop as a teacher. Trying to take the teaching ideas that fitted my ideology, but also the one that I knew worked well.

I was lucky that I still had contact with my old middle school head teacher and emailed him about career advice. He invited me to visit his school for a meeting and by the end of the meeting he had planned how I was going to get my teaching degree part time whilst working at his school as a member of support staff. I've never looked back, and I am now approaching my tenth year in the school!

Having worked through a variety of positions from support staff, to HLTA to experienced year 6 teacher: I have seen a lot in my ten years. I have seen certain fads in teaching come and go already, the 'fluffy' ideas that enter the teaching industry which claim to be the 'be all and end all' solution to everything - when really they aren't.

I chose to join Jamie in writing this mini guide for newly qualified teachers largely because this is the kind of real life, no-nonsense-book I looked for but could never find. Too many teaching advice books cram themselves with so much theory, which isn't as useful for you now - compared to when you are training! This book is purely experience, and is written based on what we know works for us, and what we know can work for you as well.

Contact

Twitter – @MrOzzyMaths

Instagram - @worthingdad

Jamie Parkinson

I grew up in Worthing, West Sussex and have lived and worked here ever since! When I was at Middle School, my year 6 teacher told me that one day I would make a great teacher, so I decided there and then that I would do it! My path to teaching has been an ambiguous one, as has my career in education since I started.

I left High School with all of my GCSE grades before studying English Language and Literature, as well as Drama, at Chichester College. Whilst studying at college I gained some school experience in a local school but I was at a stage where another four years in education to complete my training just didn't appeal.

Unsure about the path I wanted to pursue, I decided to take some time out of education and work for a little while. I discussed this with lecturers at college and found that they had vacancies for Learning Assistants in a department that dealt with children who had been excluded from their High Schools. Whilst knowing it would be challenging, I felt this job would give me a grounding financially and ultimately answer the question as to whether I had it in me to complete my teacher training.

I worked as a Learning Assistant for a year before becoming an Instructor teaching QCA units in English and maths. As much as I enjoyed my time with the children, who were mightily challenging at times, I never really had a career path in Further Education that I could follow without my degree. I looked into Primary Education again and realised that the course at the University of

Chichester was actually only 3 years – result. I took the decision there and then to jump and give it a go. I haven't looked back since.

I qualified in 2007 and took up my first teaching post in the September of that year. Throughout my NQT year I took a keen interest in ICT and the development of the school's curriculum, with a view to leading the development of ICT in my second year. As circumstances changed in the five-form-entry school, I actually became a Year Leader in my second year, as well as taking up the responsibility of ICT Co-Ordinator! When I was first informed I was ecstatic, but also rather scared as it all sunk in!

I had really enjoyed my NQT year and had really got involved with as much as I could. I wanted to be a successful teacher, but I wanted to enjoy the children's success in all of the extra-curricular activities they had been doing as well. As a Year Leader I was involved in leading Performance Management, completing lesson observations, taking year group and upper school assemblies and presenting at Governors Meetings – to name but a few!

I remained Year 4 Leader for three years before moving to Year 7, as the school followed the old middle school format at this time. I remained head of Year 7 for three further years before taking up my current role of E-Learning Leader and Pupil Premium Champion. I am now focussing on developing our school curriculum using 21st century technology under one umbrella, and focussing on improving the academic opportunities and performance of disadvantaged children under another umbrella!

I have chosen to write this book with Luke because I feel other literature in the education field can be too 'wordy' when all I would have liked when I was an NQT was a book that was usefully structured but that would have been a key resource that I would have returned to at various times!

Thank you for taking the time to share our experiences and I hope you have enjoyed the content of this book!

Contact
Twitter - @MrP_Teaches